Beastly Bristol

The book for Brave and Adventurous Children

Julian Lea-Jones

To my grandson Danny who, on a day out in Bristol,
first drew my attention to some of the creatures
peering at us from high up on the buildings.
Finding the answers to his questions provided
the inspiration for this book.

A happy collaboration between:
© Julian, Daniel Lea Jones and Oliver Ledbury for the photographs
© Meera Joshi for the Rhymes
© Kevin Powell (Kip) for the Caricatures
© Foreword by Douglas Merritt
© Julian Lea-Jones 2006

First published in 2006 by Redcliffe Press Ltd.,
81g Pembroke Road, Bristol BS8 3EA

www.redcliffepress.co.uk
www.childrensbristol.co.uk

ISBN 1 904537 52 9
ISBN 13 9781904537526
British Library Cataloguing-in-Publication Data
A catalogue record for this book is available from the British Library.
All rights reserved. Except for the purpose of review, no part of this book may be reproduced,
stored in a retrieval system, or transmitted, in any form or by any means, electronic, mechanical,
photocopying, recording or otherwise, without the prior permission of the publishers.
Design and typesetting by Stephen Morris Communications, smc@freeuk.com
Printed by Gutenberg Press Ltd, Malta

Contents

A few words from the Professor 4

You are being watched! 5

An A to Z of Bristol beasts 6

The Beastly Hunters Adventure 33

Beastly Hunting in the City 58

Beastly Hunting around Clifton 60

Where the beasts are hiding (Gazetteer) 62

Quiz answers 74

Some animal addresses – a challenge! 75

Further reading and websites 76

Acknowledgements 78

The Children's Bristol Series 79

A few words from the Professor

What an amusing discovery!

While exploring Bristol with his young grandson, Julian Lea-Jones found almost as many birds, beasts, insects and reptiles hiding in the streets as there are inside Bristol's famous zoo. Who would have thought there was a menagerie lying-in-wait for unsuspecting pedestrians? A seal, a python, a mosquito, monkeys – and many more. The creatures that Julian's sharp eye encountered are presented here, with great enthusiasm, in pages rather than cages. Following the author you can track them and *Beastly Bristol* will encourage the capture of some that may have escaped his attention. Bristol Zoo has been on the same site since 1836 – the year Queen Victoria was told she was to be Queen of England. Even she would have been amused to know so many animals appear to have escaped.

By happy chance the city is also the home of other members of the animal kingdom, with many Bristol accents, created by Aardman for their *Creature Comforts* animations. The largest beasts you will find are the two unicorns prancing on the roof of the Council House. They are there because unicorns were added to Bristol's common seal in 1591. On hearing the words *common seal* Julian might panic, thinking he had missed an item for his ever-expanding collection. When the unicorns arrived, half-a-century ago, they were a complete surprise. The architect 'forgot' to tell the Councillors he had commissioned two 3.5 metre-high, one-ton, bronze animals. A Bristol newspaper said they were *lantern jawed, wild-eyed, and stiff-legged* but their gilded extravagance has added to the city's skyline. The day they were hoisted-up there were cheers from the crowd who first saw them. The Lord Mayor has a small unicorn, the sculptor's model, in his parlour.

There are even sculpted beasts inside Bristol Zoo. Near the restaurant is a white marble carving of a woman holding a lamb and David Wynne's large bronze of a flying mute swan graces another of the garden spaces. A bronze head of Alfred the gorilla commemorates this much-loved resident.

Tiring a little, towards the end of his task, Julian commented he had begun to count wild animals rather than sheep. Few readers will fall asleep when wandering among the flocks and herds he has gathered. If anyone does, what more pleasant way could there be of drifting into dreams from the familiar hills, squares and riversides of Bristol, a newly-discovered townscape filled with fauna?

Douglas Merritt

Did you realize that when you walk around Bristol you are being

watched?

Hundreds of animals are watching you, some from rooftops, and others are hiding around corners or even peering from the pavements!

Some of the animals are *very* strange, others are *very* fierce – but all, from aardvarks to zebras, can be found on our streets. To see them, visit the Beastly Bristol website.

Some of the amazing creatures are watching you from the very tops of buildings, and a pair of binoculars will help you see some of the details.
You probably won't find any frogs in Frogmore Street – we couldn't find a single one (was there ever a cow in Milk Street?) but I'm sure that if you look hard enough you will find some very clever cats at Catbrain Hill, and there is still an alphabet of amazing animals to be found everywhere else in Bristol.

All of you should begin here because our
Bristol streets Conceal an Alphabet of
Cats and Canaries,
Droves of Dragons, wine loving
Elephants,
Fountains full of Fish,
Gi-Normous Giraffes and perhaps a very new Gnu,
Herds of Horses, an
Itch of Insects, a
Jump of Kangaroos – yes there really is more than one! Even Antipodean
Kiwis,
Lots and lots of Lions – A Pride in our City?
Mobile-phone toting Monkeys, the bearers of sad messages,
Nice
Owls, and
Pussycats – did they really sail from Bristol? Pelicans, even a Red-Hot
    Phoenix (for Harry Potter Fans),
Queer and weird creatures – have you seen the Quetzal?
Revealed if you know how to look,
Search out
Turtles and Tortoises,
Unicorns abound and even
Viper Fish with terrible teeth, and
Whales, and finally,
X is for all the 'xtinct creatures we couldn't find, not even a
Yak and of course X is also for Crossing, which is where you'll find
Zebras.

is for
Aardvark

A is for aardvark,

For ants he'll wait,

They're his favourite snack,

That tastes so great.

b is for Beetle

B is for beetle,

Not the music kind you know,

This one's an insect,

Who's been put up for show.

C
is for Caterpillar

C is for caterpillar,

Guarding the school,

Crawling with colour,

He's super cool.

d is for Dragon

D is for dragon,

Huge ferocious things,

Fire-breathing creatures,

With giant scaly wings.

e is for Elephant

E is for elephant,

This one pretty in pink,

Its size and colour,

Make it rather distinct.

F is for fox,

Smooth, Sleek and Sly,

Aesop makes it very clear

We shouldn't trust this guy.

f is for Fox

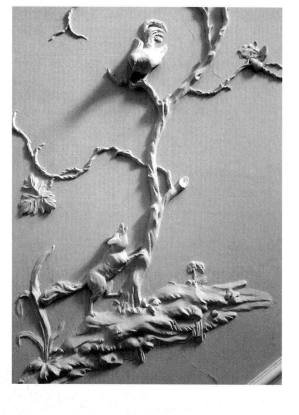

This carving tells the story of one of Aesop's famous fables 'The Fox and the Crow'. A crow flew into a cottage window, took a piece of cheese she saw upon a table, and flew up in a tree to eat it. A hungry fox seated on the ground saw this, and thought of a way to get the cheese all for himself. He began complimenting the crow on her beauty, and on the glossiness of her feathers. The crow was very pleased, but went on pecking away at the delicious piece of cheese. The fox then said,

I'm sure that your voice is as beautiful as the rest of you, but what saddens me is that I have never been lucky enough to hear the song of such a beautiful creature.

The silly crow, flattered by the fox's false praise immediately opened her beak to sing – and of course you can guess what happened next – the cheese fell down to the ground where it was quickly gobbled up by the fox!

The moral of this tale is clear, if people flatter you and praise you too highly – more than in your heart you know is justified – be careful. Ask yourself

why are they doing it?

But while being careful, be thankful and gracious in accepting praise that is due for something that you have done well.

G is for goose,

Laying fantastic golden eggs,

With feathers soft and white,

And short squatty legs.

g is for Goose

h is for Horse

H is for horse,

Racing as fast as light,

If one charged towards you,

It would give you a fright.

Could these be the famous horses of the Camargue coast in southern France? They were written about in a poem by Roy Campbell with the lines *Will never rest until...breathes the foam and hears the native thunder of the deep.* Or perhaps one of them is even Black Beauty, running free with friends, as told in the story by Anna Sewell.

I is for Iguana

I is for iguana,

Scary and green,

A lazy lizard,

With a scaly sheen.

J is for Jaguar

J is for jaguar,

Agile and speedy,

Its fur smooth and soft,

Its eyes dark and beady.

K is for Kangaroo

K is for kangaroo,
Who hops around,
When she's really on the go,
She barely touches ground.

L is for Lion

L is for lion,

A wild ferocious beast,

With a frizzy mane and glaring eyes,

Searching for a feast.

m is for Mice

M is for mice,

Hiding from cats,

Small grey and furry,

And cuter than rats.

n is for Nautilus

N is for nautilus,

In a fossil small and swirly,

Also found in water,

With a shell that's round and whirly.

This is a fossilised nautilus called an ammonite and is millions of years old.

 is for Ostrich

O is for ostrich,

The largest bird on land,

When faced with danger,

His head goes in the sand.

p is for Parrot

P is for parrots,

The birds that talk,

When people pass by,

They may even squawk.

 is for Quetzal

Q is for quetzal,
An endangered bird,
Symbolising freedom,
So I've heard.

r is for Rabbit

R is for rabbits,

Bouncing on the grass,

Hopping and playing happily,

But hiding if people pass.

S is for Snail

S is for snail,

With its home on its back,

So frail and delicate,

So easy to crack.

T is for Turtle

T is for turtle,
With a valuable shell,
So deep in the ocean
He likes to dwell.

U is for Unicorn

U is for unicorn,

With a grand golden horn,

But this mythical creature

Was never really born.

The Lion and the Unicorn were fighting for the Crown.
The Lion beat the Unicorn, all around the town.
Some gave them white bread, some gave them brown.
Some gave them plum cake and drummed them out of town.

Poem attributed to William King, about 1708-9

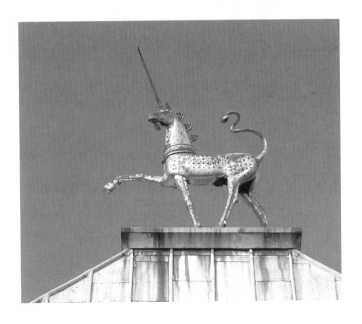

V is for Viper fish

V is for viper fish,

A hideous beast,

An unsightly creature

To say the least.

W is for Whale

W is for whale,

From the bottom of the sea,

Hanging on a shop

Is not where he should be!

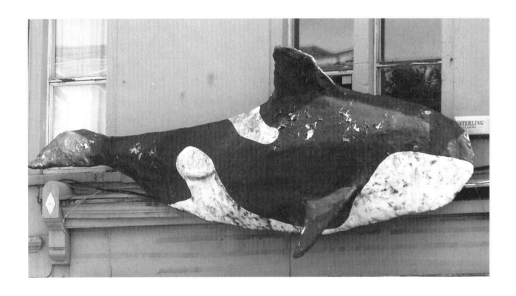

X is for Extinct – which is why there is no X

We've lost nearly 800 species of animals in the past 500 years. Many more are endangered, such as the hawksbill turtle, the snow leopard and the golden lion tamarin. Over 15,500 species face extinction today. You can help save them by joining a conservation charity such as WWF which is dedicated to helping endangered species and threatened habitats.

Look at websites such as:

www.wwf.org.uk

www.iucn.org

www.extinct.petermaas.nl

www.travellog.com/guatemala/quetzal.html

Y is for Yak which we haven't found yet.

Have you?

And finally...

Z is for Zoo

Bristol has one of the world's great zoos, where you can see more than 400 species of animals from every part of planet Earth.

Bristol Zoo is famed for its conservation and it participates in 82 different conservation breeding programmes, including 23 for birds and 30 for mammals. The Zoo also supports worldwide campaigns for the conservation and protection of endangered animals.

Find out more at www.bristolzoo.org.uk

Here I hope you will agree

Has been the most extraordinary collection of animals

You will ever see.

Beastly Hunters!
the Adventure begins
here

We bet you didn't know there were so many animals around Bristol! Not only are they fun to look at but they are so interesting – almost every one has a story to tell.

To find out more about them, and to join in our adventure:

Follow their stories
Answer the quiz questions
Go and see the beasts for yourself!
(The maps show a selection to help you find them)

To **start** your adventure

This pyramid of animals above a pet shop in Bedminster is an example of the surprises in store for you.

Have a close look at the picture. Can you find the answers to these questions? **When you've finished all the questions turn to page 74.**

Q1 How many different sorts of creatures are there?

Q2 How many creatures are there altogether?

BEASTLY BRISTOL   33

NOW are you **brave** enough to help us find these beasts?

Scariest The viper fish with lots of horrible teeth.

Funniest Fish squirting children wanting a drink from Kate's fountain.

Fiercest The eagle watching sick pets being taken to hospital.

Jolliest
The giant caterpillar having a break from school to go to the park for a snack of grass and leaves.

Saddest
The Unicorn that has lost its horn, but is still helping the Lion.

Nastiest The monkey holding the poor cat's paw in the fire.

Smallest The mouse watching the parrots.

Biggest The brick fish falling from the sky, an amazing sight for cyclists using the Bristol & Bath Railway path!
Or is it the **heaviest**?

and the **prettiest** The Butterfly warming its wings on the school wall.

The camels that dance for JOY

These camels are dromedaries, the kind that have only one hump. If you go to Tailors' Court off Broad Street, you can see them dancing above the doorway in the coat of arms of the Merchant Tailors' Guild.

In ancient times tailors, who designed and made clothes, were very important people. They had their own trade union,

the Merchant Tailors' Guild, to make sure that they made the clothes properly. The tailors were skilled at making expensive clothes from silks and other fine cloths for knights and their ladies. The silks were brought from Arabia and Asia by trains of camels along a route known as the Silk Road. In this coat of arms you can see the eastern (Arabian) style of the tent and the exotic animals. These pictures would have reminded the tailors' customers that the material had come from faraway countries and how difficult it was to import.

What can you see in the coat of arms? The two camels, the gold lion and the tent are easy to spot but look closely.

Q3 Can you spot ten different things in the coat of arms?

BEASTLY BRISTOL   35

Monkey has just received really bad news

M is for monkey,
But with no cheeky grin,
Looking sad and low,
Is his only sin.

Surely you must have some?

I'm Sorry. Yes, we have no Bananas!

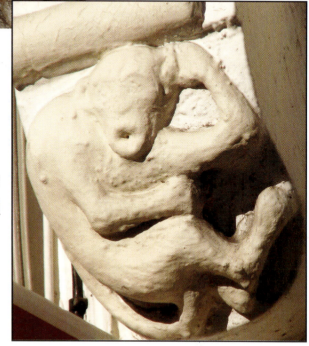

The Crow and the Pitcher

This carving illustrates one of Aesop's fables.

A clever crow was dying of thirst when it discovered a tall jug.

He flew to it hoping to find water but when he reached the jug he discovered that it contained only a small amount in the bottom. Its beak couldn't reach the water, and it did not have enough strength to overturn the jug.

What do you think the clever crow did?

It solved the problem by collecting pebbles and dropping them in one by one until the water level rose sufficiently for it to drink.

You can try this yourself with a jar with some water, and you will see that by dropping marbles into it you can get the water to rise, just as the clever crow did.

Archimedes, the famous Greek mathematician and scientist of 2,200 years ago, also discovered this theory of displacement of water, called Archimedes' principle; he got into a bath that was already full to the brim whereupon the water ran all over the sides and down through the kitchen ceiling. He was so excited that he ran into the street wearing only his bath towel, shouting *Eureka* (which is Greek for *I have found it*).

We don't suggest you try this experiment for yourself, otherwise your parents will probably shout something, and it won't be *Eureka!*

HERE BE DRAGONS

This dragon was so thirsty, it had to climb up the building to get a drink out of the rain gutter.

This Hedge Dragon in Henleaze just grew and grew, until it was big enough to eat Graham's wheely bin!

This dragon seems very friendly… until you take a close look at the very rude face at the bottom of the bracket. He has a lot of friends to help him support all the balconies in his building.

Q4 How many dragons are there holding up the balconies at King's Arcade in Boyce's Avenue?

This eagle is trying to hide from the dragon. Notice how the eagle's wings are tucked in flat against the wall, hoping that the dragon won't see it. ▼

We have noticed that dragons and other dragon-like creatures often hide above doorways like these. We are told as children not to walk on the cracks in the pavement, *in case the bears get you*, but perhaps we should check above the doorways as well – just in case there are dragons lurking there waiting to pounce! ▼▲

The dragon can't find the eagle and is so hungry that it's eating its own tail. ▼

But don't be frightened – just look what happened to this dragon that was getting ready to pounce on children going down the Zig-Zag. He got caught ▼ and slain by St George.

In olden times, before Cabot discovered North America in 1497, mapmakers making plans for explorers of new and unknown lands thought there could be many dangers and terrible things, so they added the warning on the map *Hic Sunt Dracones*, which is Latin for **Here there be Dragons**.

Gooses or GEESE?

For many years these 'gooses' (what else would you call a goose with two heads, or two geese with one body?), lived above the famous Blue Goose restaurant in Gloucester Road, Horfield. ▼

They retired to live on this house in Kingsdown.

Ever optimistic, they still keep their napkin around their necks in case they are asked to work for another restaurant.

The **CANARY** and the CAT

This canary came all the way from Norwich to see the Robins at Ashton Gate.

But when it got to Henleaze, it was told all about this fierce cat waiting for it on a roof in Chapter Street in St Pauls. The canary decided to stay here where it was safe on the roof, and where the kind children Alex, Susanna and Christian, put food out for it.

Imagine how frightened the canary would have been it had been caught by a cat as fierce as this!

A CHAMELEON watches for MOSQUITOES and other tasty insects

The chameleon (a master of disguise, can you spot him?) will do us a favour if he can catch this mosquito.

It is so strong that it has been able to pierce this metal railing – imagine the size of bite it could make on your arm!

BEASTLY BRISTOL

Lion School

This Lion Marshall is keeping a watchful eye over the pupils at Queen Elizabeth's Hospital. ▶

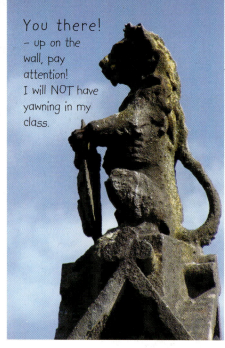

You there!
– up on the wall, pay attention! I will NOT have yawning in my class.

A lion thinking about lunch and watching people on the zebra crossing.

Big Cats

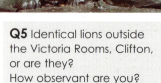

Q5 Identical lions outside the Victoria Rooms, Clifton, or are they?
How observant are you?

I've just had lunch, thank you – all those tasty people inside the restaurant.

Now we know why the lion looks smug!

◀

I had to ask them to nail the knocker down 'cos I got fed up with children playing 'knock up Ginger' and keeping me awake.

▶

a pride in our city?

Q6 How many lions are watching you from the Drill Hall?

Warning
If you sit on this bench mind you don't get your fingers bitten!

This is the former Drill Hall in Old Market Street. It is now flats where people live. ▶

BEASTLY BRISTOL 43

Unicorn and Friend

When you are hunting for creatures around the city, look out for coats of arms. There are lots and lots!

On the Bristol coat of arms there are two unicorns holding each side of the shield, with a ship and a castle in the middle. The ship and castle are also on the front face of the city seal. The castle probably represents the castle built by William the Conqueror during the eleventh century and the ship indicates that Bristol was an important and prosperous medieval seaport.

If the animals supporting the shield are a lion and a unicorn, it is the Royal Coat of Arms. You can see that the shield is topped by the royal crown.

> **Q7** What is strange about the unicorn on the Royal Coat of Arms shown above?

Bristol's coat of arms has two unicorns supporting it.
This can be seen (above) on the former Drill Hall, Old Market.

The coat of arms above the doorway of the Guildhall in Broad Street shows the reverse side of the city seal – a trumpeter on the battlements of the castle.

BEARS

Have you ever been warned not to walk on the cracks in the pavement, 'in case the bears get you'?

This bear has had his plan foiled because Peter took Sarah's hand and made sure that she avoided the really wide crack in the pavement.

The other bears at the zoo who don't try and trick children in this way are happy that Peter was able to protect Sarah, and are rolling around with happiness.

Flocks of Birds

When a visitor from abroad was asked why it came, it replied: *The Polygon.*

No, not where, I meant why?

That's what I said, because Polly's gone.

Look there she goes.

Clever Stork outwits the Fox

You watch my back and I'll watch yours.

Where has that pigeon gone?

I'm sure I saw it a minute ago!

I must do better because I'm paid to chase the pigeons away.

A FISHY BUSINESS

Kate Malone's happy fish. Mind it doesn't squirt you in the eye!

You strange, astonished-looking, angle-faced..

From *To a Fish*, a poem by James Henry Leigh Hunt.

And a very unhappy fish, leaping into the sky to escape the fish and chip fryer.

A star fish...

...and a fish that fell from the stars?

A fish that stings and...

... a very spiky fish from the deep.

BEASTLY BRISTOL 47

A sorry tail or the mouse with a tale to tell?

I wonder what on earth has happened to the unicorn's tail to make the unicorn so cross?

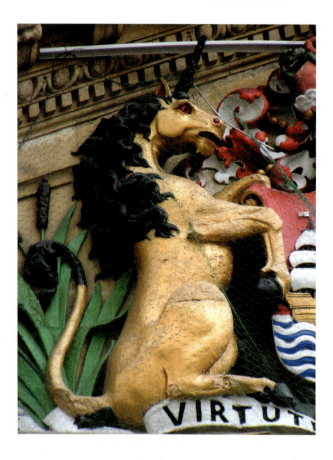

Well, wouldn't you be cross if a mouse bit your bottom?

A School of Dolphins

A School of Dolphins – and there are even more around Bristol. Are they studying for their GCSEs – Grand Certificate in Swimming Expertise?

D is for dolphin,

Skimming through the sea,

Splashing and spraying,

As happy as can be.

BEASTLY BRISTOL

The FOX and the STORK

Jean de la Fontaine was a French poet who, in the seventeenth century, wrote a series of fables like those of Aesop. This fable tells of the fox who invited a lady friend, Madame Stork for dinner.

The surprising results of two invitations

However, the crafty fox served up a dinner of soup in this shallow dish. The poor stork with her long beak could not get anything to eat.

But look at the second carving to see how Madame Stork got her revenge.

The stork invited the fox back for dinner and served it up in this long necked jar.

However hard he tried, the crafty fox couldn't reach the food, while the stork with her long beak could easily reach the food – so it was his turn to go hungry.

The moral of this tale is that people who try to cheat others are often outsmarted by the intended victim.

The Monkeys, the Cat, the Wolf and the Fox

The carving above depicts a fable in which the monkey flattered the cat in order to get it to steal hot chestnuts from the fire at the risk of burning its paws. You can see in this carving that the cat changes its mind, but too late. Maybe the monkey is one of the spiteful Bandar-log that Rudyard Kipling wrote about in *The Jungle Book*.

The moral of this tale is don't let people flatter you into doing things that are wrong – you may end up getting hurt.

Don't be discouraged, not all monkeys are like this. The monkey in the next picture plays a very different part – that of a judge.

The carving below shows a fable from the second book. In this fable, the monkey acted as a Judge (the scales in his paw represent the balance of justice), when a wolf, on the right, accused a fox, on the left, of stealing something. The monkey decided that both the sly fox and the wicked wolf were guilty in their own way, which explains why they are raising their paws angrily to the monkey. The lesson is that someone who accuses someone else of a wrongdoing may sometimes be guilty, and is just using the false accusation to cover up their own misdeed.

In this old carving the fox's face is damaged making him look like a cat.

BEASTLY BRISTOL 51

Lots of Dogs

Danny's dogs, Bob and Bill are enjoying a swim on a hot summer day.

Is Jasmine lost At-Bristol or just thinking *Where on earth have Bob and Bill gone now?*

Dogs fighting.

Dog barking at a bird in the tree.

Is Nipper listening to his master's voice, or is he really listening to his MP3 player?

D is for Dog,
Nipper's his name,
As a global trademark,
He's not short of fame.

An Antipodean Menagerie

Kanga and Roo visiting the Eye Hospital.

They misread the sign – they thought it said Eeyore Hospital. Although they were pleased to learn that he wasn't in hospital, they were still worried about Eeyore. So Kanga hopped on a bus up to Clifton to take Roo to Bristol Zoo to visit her cousin, to see if he knew where Eeyore was.

Kanga's Clifton cousin.

On the way to the zoo they met another friend from Australia, a Duck-Billed Platypus. They asked him:

What on earth are you doing climbing over someone's garden fence?

He said he had been told that Julian had a nice big pond to swim in, but as he couldn't find it he would join them on their trip to the zoo where he knew they had a lovely lake.

Although Kanga, Roo, and 'Platty' had a lovely time at the zoo, there was still no sign of Eeyore so they decided to go back to their friends in Brislington. The friend that they were staying with introduced them to another visitor, *Kiwi*, also from the Antipodes. This visitor was quite old – he had come to England from New Zealand in the 1940s and had liked Bristol so much that he decided to stay.

A PHOENIX with her YOUNG tries to rise from the ashes

I know the Firemen mean to help but how can I be re-born if they keep putting me out?

I'll have to ask my friend Harry if he can talk to them for me.

splendidly sinuous Serpent

Why helloooo there, my name is Kaa the Rock Python. You look like a nice child.

Wouldn't you like to visit me? I'm really very friendly, I won't hurt you.

You may have read about me in *The Jungle Book* by Rudyard Kipling.

Oh dear! Can you help me? I've suddenly got a terrible headache.

BEASTLY BRISTOL 55

More Mythical Beasts

Does this Centaur have the job of showing people the way to the centre?
A centaur is a creature in Greek mythology. It is half-man and half-horse.

A sphinx is a winged creature with a human face and the body of a lion.
This sphinx looks very thin. Is it because Oedipus solved her riddle? There is a classical myth that the sphinx guarded the gates of Thebes, in Greece, allowing no one to enter or leave the city without answering the following riddle:

> What is the animal that goes on four feet in the morning, on two at midday and upon three in the evening?

If the traveller could not answer correctly, she would kill and devour him. As no one had yet come up with the right answer, the sphinx was well-fed. However, Oedipus solved the puzzle and told everyone the answer so she couldn't catch anyone else to eat.

Look, you've gone and got mud all over your back again. What on earth will Mum say?

Q8 Do you know the answer to the sphinx's riddle?

A griffin has the head and wings of an eagle and the body of a lion.
In ancient mythology, griffins were seen as the guardians of treasure and they are shown here guarding golden bezants, the very valuable gold coins of Byzantium.

The Happy Seal with a story to tell and the very unhappy fish

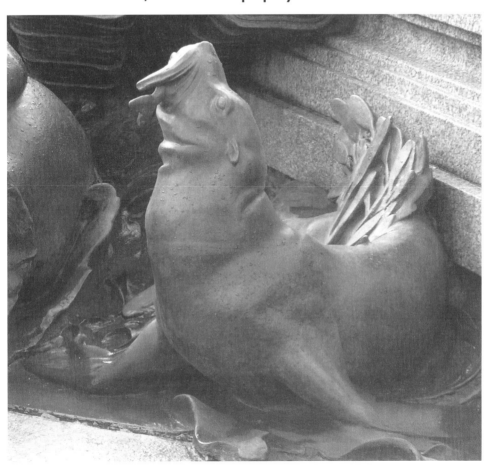

❛ On 6 September 2005 the *Bristol Evening Post* published a letter which asked why one of my fellow seals had swum up the River Avon and as far as the Feeder canal at Netham. The ignorant humans even had the cheek to call him *Whitby* without even asking him what his name was.

Absolute impertinence! If the reporter had asked me the question I would have told him. I invited him to come to taste the marvellous fish in my fountain. Also his name isn't *Whitby*, its *Solomon* (the wise old seal). ❜

Beastly hunting in the city

Where to find some of the beasts

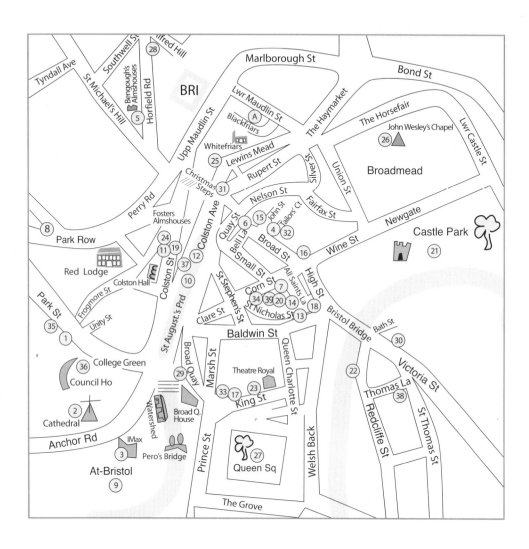

A   Bristol Eye Hospital, Lower Maudlin Street: aardvark, ant, flying bird, birds, butterfly, daddy long legs, dragonfly, earthworm, elephant, fish, flea, giraffe, hedgehog, jellyfish, kangaroo, mayfly, millipede, mongoose, mosquito, pig, scorpion, snail, spider, tortoise
1   Two beasts, Park Street
2   Ape, Elder Lady Chapel, Bristol Cathedral
3   Beetle, Anchor Square
4   Camels, Tailors' Court
5   Centaur, Horfield Road
6   Cockerel, St John's Church, Broad Street
7   Dinosaur, All Saints Lane entrance in The Exchange
8   Dog, Park Row/Woodland Road
9   Dog, Millennium Square
10 Dolphin, St Augustine's Parade
11 Dolphin, Colston Hall, Colston Street
12 Dolphins, Colston Avenue
13 Dolphins, St Nicholas Steps
14 Dragon, St Nicholas Parade
15 Dragon, Everard Building, St John's Lane
16 Dragon, Christ Church, Broad Street
17 Dragon, Merchant Seamen's Almshouses, King Street
18 Eagle, St Nicholas Parade
19 Eagle, Colston Hall, Colston Street
20 Elephant, 20 St Nicholas Street
21 Fish, Castle Park
22 Fish, opposite Welsh Back/King Street on Redcliffe harbourside
23 Griffins, 33 King Street
24 Hawk, Colston Hall, Colston Street
25 Horse, Lewins Mead
26 Horse, John Wesley's Chapel, Broadmead
27 Horse and William III, Queen Square
28 Leopard, the Green, Horfield Road
29 Lion, outside Broad Quay House
30 Lion, Victoria Street
31 Lions, Colston Avenue
32 Mermaids, (possibly) Tailors' Court
33 Mermaid, Merchant Seamen's Almshouses, King Street
34 Penguin, west entrance, in The Exchange
35 Rams, Freemasons Hall, Park Street
36 Sea horses, Council House, College Green
37 Sheep, Colston Street
38 Sheep, St Thomas Street
39 Unicorn, old stock exchange, St Nicholas Street

Beastly hunting around Clifton

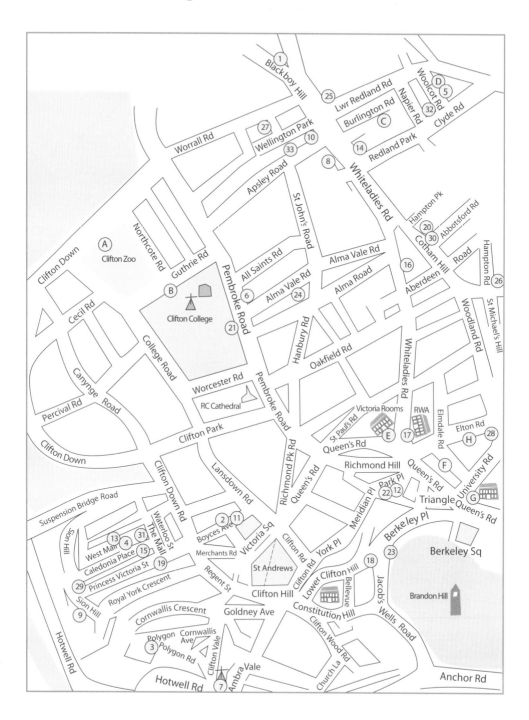

A   Bristol Zoo, Clifton Down: lots of beasts above the entrance, from bears to tigers
B   Clifton College, Guthrie Road: a dragon, a lion and fiendish friends
C   18 Burlington Road: a menagerie in iron, from an armadillo to a viper fish
D   Woolcot Road: look out for a monkey, an owl and a pigeon over the shops
E   Victoria Rooms, Queen's Road: lions and aquatic creatures abound
F   9-11 Elmdale Road, a hare, monkey and others
G   Browns Restaurant, Queen's Road, a monkey, a pelican, a ram and friends
H   Bristol Grammar School, Elton Road, bees, griffins, and horses
1   Bear, men's toilet, Blackboy Hill
2   Beastly creatures, King's Arcade, Boyce's Avenue
3   Bird, Polygon
4   Birds, bootscrapers, West Mall
5   Cat, Old Barn, Woolcot Road
6   Dolphins, All Saints Church, Pembroke Road
7   Dove, Holy Trinity Church, Hotwells
8   Dove, St John's Church Hall, Whiteladies Road
9   Dragon, Prince's Buildings, Sion Hill
10 Dragonfly, St John's Church, Apsley Road
11 Dragons, King's Arcade, Boyce's Avenue
12 Goat, Pro-Cathedral, Park Place
13 Griffin, bootscrapers, West Mall
14 Fish, Colley's Supper Rooms, 153 Whiteladies Road
15 Hawks, Caledonia Place
16 Iguana, 89 Whiteladies Road
17 Lion and unicorn, RWA, Queen's Road
18 Lion, roof, Berkeley Place
19 Maybug, Princess Victoria Street
20 Owl, over shop, Cotham Hill
21 Quetzal, 81g Pembroke Road
22 Scorpion, Pro-Cathedral, Park Place
23 Sea horses, QEH gates, Lower Berkeley Road
24 Seagull, weathervane, Alma Vale Road
25 Sheep, 3 Lower Redland Road
26 Snakes, balconies, Cotham Road
27 Snakes, rear of Anglesey Place
28 Snake, on bench at Bristol Grammar School, Woodland Road
29 Sphinx, St Vincent's Priory, Sion Hill
30 Stork, over shop, Cotham Hill
31 Unicorns, lamp post, The Mall
32 Unicorns, lamp posts, Clyde Road
33 Woodpecker, 59 Apsley Road

Where the beasts are hiding

This next section is a gazetteer of the locations of all the Bristol Beasts that we have discovered so far, together with some interesting facts we found out about many of the beasts. Creatures illustrated in this book are shown in bold. You can find some of them on the maps on pages 58 and 60.

There is a whole farmyard of animals for you to find – sheep, rams, goats, cows, horses and even a mother pig. There are mini-beasts, bugs and creepy-crawlies too and spiders, snails, daddy long legs, a millipede, bees (with their own beehive), and even an earthworm, are just waiting to be discovered.

But while you are looking out for these, don't forget all the other wild creatures that are still out there for you to find – creatures such as crocodiles, dinosaurs, armadillos, scorpions; gorillas, a bat, a lynx, an elk, a bison, jellyfish and even a mongoose.

A devil at Lansdown Villas?

A pair of terrible beasts with no name – the very worst sort, snarling and sticking their tongues out at each other, on the College Green end wall, beneath the neon sign for the Mauretania at the bottom of Park Street.

A thoughtful beast watching passers-by (but what is it thinking?). Lansdown Villas, 120 Kellaway Avenue, Golden Hill, Horfield (possibly modelled on the 'Stonegate devil' in York).

Aardvark. The Creation plaque by Walter Ritchie, 1986, Bristol Eye Hospital, Lower Maudlin Street.

> **Q9** How many different sorts of creatures can you count on the creation plaque (and don't forget the flea)?

Ammonite. Ammonites lived millions and millions of years ago. They belonged to a group known as cephalopods and nautili (sea snails) which exist today are very similar to ammonites. The name nautilus comes from the Greek nautilus, which means 'sailor'. Pliny, the most important naturalist in antiquity, named its flat spiral shell 'Ammonis Cornu', Jupiter's Horn. This one is set in the front garden wall of a house at Dowry Parade, Hotwells Road.

Animal mask. Plaster frieze in the entrance hall of the Royal Fort House, Tyndall Avenue.

Ant. The Creation plaque by Walter Ritchie, 1986, Bristol Eye Hospital, Lower Maudlin Street.

Ape. Playing panpipes, beside one of the arches in the Elder Lady Chapel, Bristol Cathedral. This carving is over 700 years old. To give you an idea how long ago that is, it is about the time your great, great (x 22), grandparents were alive!

Armadillo. Metal sculpture by Julian Warren, on his railings at 18 Burlington Road, Redland.

Bat. Metal sculpture by Julian Warren, on his railings at 18 Burlington Road, Redland.

Bear. On a pillar at Browns Restaurant, 38 Queen's Road, Clifton.

Bear. Snow white and upright at the White Bear pub, 133 St Michael's Hill, Kingsdown (watching to see if children step on the cracks in the pavement).

Bear. Watching the traffic from his place on the rainwater gutter of the men's toilet, top of Blackboy Hill, Durdham Downs. Why is its mouth open?

Bears. Frolicking, frieze above entrance to Bristol Zoo Gardens, Clifton Down Road, Clifton.

Beastly creatures. Be very, very careful, when walking along here. They are making faces at you from beneath the dragon balcony brackets, King's Arcade, Boyce's Avenue, Clifton.

Bees. Bees times three (or is it the face of a man with a moustache?) on the coat of arms on the Bristol Grammar School building fronting Elton Road, Tyndall's Park.

Bees. Above entrance to 18A Baldwin Street (O'Neill's). The motto reads 'Nothing without Labour'.

Q10 How many bees can you see at 18a Baldwin Street?

Beetle. This two-metre long rhinoceros beetle by Nicola Hicks is a bronze sculpture on a small limestone block in Anchor Square, outside Wildwalk. Rhinoceros beetles are the strongest animals on the planet, they can carry up to 850 times their own weight! That is the equivalent of a man carrying over 70 cars on his back.

Bird. Above ground floor windows of 9–11 Elmdale Road, Tyndall's Park.

Bird and Man. Frieze at E Shed, Canons Road, city centre. Why are they trying to outstare each other?

Flying Bird. Above a statue of Saint Odilia, Inner Courtyard of Bristol Eye Hospital, Lower Maudlin Street. Sculpted by Stephen Joyce in 1985. The plaque inside the hospital tells you about Saint Odilia and the reason for making this statue and putting it here.

Bird. Polygon, Clifton.

Birds. Hawks on boot scrapers, West Mall, Clifton.

Birds. The Creation plaque by Walter Ritchie, 1986, Bristol Eye Hospital, Lower Maudlin Street.

Bison. Frieze above entrance to Bristol Zoo Gardens, Clifton Down Road, Clifton.

Bug. Temple Square, Temple Quay.

Butterfly. The Creation plaque by Walter Ritchie, 1986, Bristol Eye Hospital, Lower Maudlin Street.

Butterfly. Victoria Park Community Infant School, St John's Lane, Bedminster.

Camel. The Bactrian camel, originally from Bactria in central Asia, easily recognisable because it has two humps. Frieze above entrance to Bristol Zoo Gardens, Clifton Down Road, Clifton.

Camels. Prancing in Tailors' Court, off Broad Street. The camel with only one hump is a Dromedary, is Arabian and was bred for its speed.

Canary. Roof ridge of 44 Holmes Grove, Henleaze. This is the canary that came all the way from Norwich to see the Robins at Bristol City.

Cat. Being forced to take the hot chestnuts out of the fire for the monkey, carved panel, above ground-floor windows of 10 Elmdale Road, Tyndall's Park.

Cats. Balancing on dogs, pet shop menagerie, Pets Plus, 27a East Street, Bedminster. This pyramid of animals was designed by Pete Milner of ACESS as part of a City and Community Art project to revitalize the Bedminster Shopping area.

Cat. On the roof parapet of The Old Barn, Woolcot Road, Redland (placed there by the former owner, the late Reverend Springett-Nicholson).

Cat. Above roof parapet of a house in Chapter Street, St Pauls.

Caterpillar. Victoria Park Community Infant School, St John's Lane, Bedminster.

Centaur. Plaque, Horfield Road, Kingsdown.

Chameleon. Catching an insect. Metal sculpture by Julian Warren, on his railings at 18 Burlington Road, Redland.

Cockerel. This one is on the steeple of St John's Church, Broad Street; notice that it even has a red comb on its head like a proper rooster.

Cow. One of many medieval carvings of animals and strange beasts on the pillars beside the North Porch of St Mary Redcliffe Church. Inside the church you can see a real rib-bone of a whale. Feel your own rib bone and then look at this one to realize how big the whale must have been!

Cow's head, high above the memorial fountain, Stoke Road, Durdham Down.

Crocodile. 'Africa' plaque above the south entrance, The Exchange, Corn Street.

Crow. Crow and the pitcher, first panel above the ground floor windows of 10 Elmdale Road, Tyndall's Park.

Crow. Being tricked out of its lunch by the fox's flattery. Stairwell, Royal Fort House, Tyndall Avenue.

Crow. Metal sculpture by Julian Warren, on his railings at 18 Burlington Road, Redland.

Daddy long legs (Crane Fly). The Creation plaque by Walter Ritchie, 1986, Bristol Eye Hospital, Lower Maudlin Street.

Dinosaur. 'Asia' plaque above east exit from The Exchange, All Saints Lane, Corn Street (co-existing with a camel – improbable but true!).

Dog. A stone carving of Nipper, a world-famous Bristol dog, on a ledge on the corner of Park Row and Woodland Road. Born in 1884, Nipper was the terrier owned by Mark Barraud, a scenic artist at the Prince's Theatre. He was painted by Mark's brother Paul watching his master and listening to an old-fashioned clockwork record player with a brass horn instead of loudspeakers. This painting was used by His Master's Voice record company (known today as HMV) as their trademark label. Nipper lived at the Princes Theatre that was destroyed by bombing in the Second World War. The theatre used to be opposite where Nipper's statue can be seen today, on the site of the former Coliseum. The statue and adjacent commemorative plaque were placed here by the Bristol Civic Society as this is the nearest spot to where Nipper lived.

Dogs. Jasmine, Bill and Bob, three life-size bronze Jack Russell terriers by Cathie Pilkington, 2000, Millennium Square, Harbourside. They were designed by Cathie as part of the revitalization of the harbourside.

Dogs. Fighting, Foster's Almshouse, Colston Street.

Dolphin. In Neptune's grasp. Neptune was the God of the Sea. St Augustine's Parade, Centre, attributed to John Rendall. This statue has been moved six times since it was originally unveiled in Temple Street in 1723.

Dog. Barking at a bird in a tree, stairwell, Royal Fort House, Tyndall Avenue.

Dolphin. Biting anchor flukes, pillar capitals, Colston Hall, Colston Street.

Dolphins. Four dolphins, one on each corner of the statue of Edward Colston, on the paved traffic island in Colston Avenue, city centre, formerly known as Magpie Park. The dolphin and an anchor were adopted as the personal emblems of Edward Colston; one of the plaques on the base of the statue illustrates the legend that Colston was saved at sea by a dolphin which became jammed in the hole when his ship sprang a leak in a storm. The statue was sculpted by John Cassidy, November 1895 and made at Coalbrookdale, Shropshire.

Dolphins. Two of four dolphins on a war memorial at All Saints Church, Pembroke Road, Clifton.

Dolphins. Above the former fish market entrance at St Nicholas Steps, St Nicholas Street. There are enough around the centre to make up a complete school of dolphins. I wonder if they come down off the buildings late at night when everyone has gone home and practise their swimming skills in the water on the centre?

Dove. Over the doorway of Holy Trinity Church, Hotwells.

Dove. With an olive branch, above doorway to St John's Church Hall, Whiteladies Road (the Britannia Building Society). This represents the Biblical dove that returned to Noah in the Ark with an olive twig to show him that it had found dry land and that the flood was over.

Doves. On a pillar at Browns Restaurant, 38 Queen's Road, Clifton.

Dragon. Above shop (writhing to escape, or is it green with envy?), St Marks Road, Easton. Dragonswell Road, in Henbury gets its name from a field on Westmoreland farm where there was a pond that never froze over because it was fed by a warm spring. However, according to local legend, the spring was kept warm by a giant dragon living in its depths (like the Loch Ness Monster).

Dragons. Along the frontage of St Nicholas Parade, St Nicholas Street. If you look closely you will see that one is so hungry it is biting its own tail.

Dragon. Frieze at E Shed, Canons Road, city centre.

Dragon. Edward Everard Building, the former Everard Printing Works, St John's Lane off Broad Street. (This one is obviously very thirsty.)

Dragon. On a weather vane, Christ Church spire, Broad Street.

Dragon. Poised for flight, roof parapet of Clifton College, Guthrie Road, Clifton.

Dragon. A very red dragon, being slain by St George. Prince's Buildings, Sion Hill, Clifton.

Dragon. With four legs. Merchant Venturers' coat of arms, Merchant Seamen's Almshouses, King Street.

Dragonfly. The Creation plaque by Walter Ritchie, 1986, Bristol Eye Hospital, Lower Maudlin Street.

Dragonfly. By Julian Warren, 59 Apsley Road, Clifton (Rucola restaurant).

Dragon-like creature. 9–11 Elmdale Road, Tyndall's Park.

Dragons. Above the left and right side of the historic St John's Church on Apsley Road, Clifton (Dreweatt Neate, auctioneers).

Dragons. Forty-eight dragons as balcony brackets, King's Arcade, Boyce's Avenue, Clifton.

Duck-billed platypus. Metal sculpture by Julian Warren, on his railings at 18 Burlington Road, Redland.

Eagle. Along frontage of St Nicholas Parade, St Nicholas Street (anxiously watching out for dragons).

Eagle. On a pillar at Browns Restaurant, 38 Queen's Road, Clifton.

Eagle. Stretching its wings on top of a pillar in front of Colston Hall, Colston Street.

Eagles. Very predatory, perhaps looking out for a pigeon for lunch? Zetland Road, Redland.

Earthworm. The Creation plaque by Walter Ritchie, 1986, Bristol Eye Hospital, Lower

peering out of the wall on the frontage of The Elephant, 20 St Nicholas Street. The Elephant Inn was built in the seventeenth century, demolished in 1863 when the street was widened but rebuilt four years later and is still trading today.

Elephant. The Creation plaque by Walter Ritchie, 1986, Bristol Eye Hospital, Lower Maudlin Street.

Elephant. Frieze above entrance to Bristol Zoo Gardens, Clifton Down Road, Clifton.

Elephant. In the pink, Honeyfield trailers, Winterstoke Road, Bedminster.

Elephant. 'Africa' plaque above the south entrance, The Exchange, Corn Street.

Elk. Frieze above entrance to Bristol Zoo Gardens, Clifton Down Road, Clifton.

Fiendish creature. Clifton College, Guthrie Road, Clifton.

Fish. Shop sign, St Mark's Road, Easton.

Fish. The Creation plaque by Walter Ritchie, 1986, Bristol Eye Hospital, Lower Maudlin Street.

Fish. 6 metre high brick fish beside Bristol and Bath railway path (adjacent to a supermarket at Fishponds).

Fish. Being eaten by a seal, sculpture by Henry Poole, 1917. Victoria Rooms fountain, Queen's Road, Clifton.

Fish. Happy fish as a water spout. *Fish* by Kate Malone is a bronze drinking fountain at Castle Park. Kate's ceramic model is in the Bristol Museum and Art Gallery.

Fish. Fish out of water, sculpture by Henry Poole, 1917. Victoria Rooms fountain, Queen's Road, Clifton.

Fish. Trying to escape the 'fish and chip' fryer, East Street, Bedminster.

Fish. Very scary on the obelisk 'Unknown Deep', by Philippa Threlfall and Kennedy Collings, 1991. Redcliffe Quay, opposite the Welsh Back end of King Street.

Flea. A fleeing flea. The Creation plaque by Walter Ritchie, 1986, Bristol Eye Hospital, Lower Maudlin Street.

Fox. Tricking crow out of its lunch. Stairwell, Royal Fort House, Tyndall Avenue, Clifton.

Fox. Entertaining stork to dinner, from Jean de la Fontaine's fable. First side panel, 11 Elmdale Road, Tyndall's Park.

Fox. On roof edge of Old Barn, 22 Luccombe Hill, Lower Redland Road, Redland.

Fox. Being judged by monkey, above ground floor windows, 9–11 Elmdale Road, Tyndall's Park.

Fox. Carrying off a goose from the farmyard, beside one of the arches in the Elder Lady Chapel, Bristol Cathedral.

Giraffe. Frieze above entrance to Bristol Zoo Gardens, Clifton Down Road, Clifton.

Giraffe. The Creation plaque by Walter Ritchie, 1986, Bristol Eye Hospital, Lower Maudlin Street.

Gnu. A new gnu, or a bull? Temple Square, Temple Quay, off Temple Way.

Goat. On frontage arch of old Pro-Cathedral, Park Place, Clifton.

Goat. Blowing a hunting horn at the same time that it is carrying a hare on a pole over its shoulder. Beside one of the arches in Elder Lady Chapel, Bristol Cathedral.

Goat's head. High above the memorial fountain, Stoke Road, Durdham Down.

Goat's head. On a corner pillar on the frontage of Browns Restaurant, 38 Queen's Road, Clifton.

Goose. Life-sized golden goose in a 'G', pub sign at the Bristol Flyer, Gloucester Road by the old Bristol North Baths (did it come from the goose that laid the Golden Egg?).

Goose. With two heads, Bristol's famous Blue Goose, now retired to the roof parapet of house in Montague Place, Kingsdown. For years they were a landmark on the roof of Gloucester Road restaurant of the same name.

Gorilla. Frieze above entrance to Bristol Zoo Gardens, Clifton Down Road, Clifton.

Griffins. Guarding golden bezants on the coat of arms on the Bristol Grammar School building fronting Elton Road, Tyndall's Park. These were fabulous monsters, with the attributes of nobility – forequarters of a lion, the King of Beasts, the wings of an eagle, the King of Birds, and were traditional guardians of treasure. Bezants were valuable gold or silver coins from Byzantium. Also remember the griffin that was encountered by Alice in her journey through Wonderland.

Griffins. A row of six above the upper blind arcading of 33 King Street (the Raj restaurant). If you look closely you will see some are damaged. This happened as a result of bombing raids during the Second World War.

Griffin. Boot scrapers, West Mall, Clifton.

Gromit. Waiting for Wallace not Godot, by John Wyatt. 62 Upper Cranbrook Road, Redland.

Fish. Grumpy fish by Julian Warren, metal sculptor, on railings at 153 Whiteladies Road, Clifton (Colley's Supper Rooms).

Hare and Tortoise. Aesop fable, above ground floor windows, 9–11 Elmdale Road, Tyndall's Park.

Hawks. Pairs of stylised hawks as boot scrapers outside houses in Caledonia Place, Clifton.

Hawk. Flexing its wings on a pillar capital, Colston Hall, Colston Street.

Hedgehog. The Creation plaque by Walter Ritchie, 1986, Bristol Eye Hospital, Lower Maudlin Street.

Heron. Cast-iron fountain, Coalbrookdale design, Shirehampton Green.

Hedge-Dragon. It has already grown big enough to eat Graham's wheelie bin! What will it eat next? Lawrence Grove, Henleaze. This is a topiary hedge-dragon; topiary is the art of ornamental gardening where hedges are pruned into shapes. Look out for more: a topiary bird in Gayner Road and a baby dragon in the Polygon.

Hippopotamus. Frieze above entrance to Bristol Zoo Gardens, Clifton Down Road, Clifton.

Horse. 'Horse and Man' resin and bronze sculpture by Stephen Joyce, 1984, in the rear courtyard of Brunel House, St George's Road. This statue, of a horse being led by a horse trader, commemorates the site of a nineteenth-century horse-dealing centre.

Horse and rider. 'Cloaked Horseman' by sculptor David Backhouse, 1984. Outside the former St Bartholomew's Hospital, Lewins Mead.

Horse and rider. Statue of John Wesley on horseback, sculpted by A. G. Walker, 1933. The New Room, John Wesley's Chapel, Broadmead.

Horse and rider. Statue of King William III, by William Rysbrack, Queen Square. This is considered to be the finest equestrian statue in the country.

Horse's head. High above the memorial fountain, Stoke Road, Durdham Down.

Q 11 Compare this old picture postcard of the statue with the statue in Queen Square today. Can you see the difference?

From *Bygone Bristol*, Derek and Janet Fisher

Horse's Head. Parapet of Old Barn, 22 Luccombe Hill, Lower Redland Road.

Horses. Three horses racing on the coat of arms on the Bristol Grammar School building fronting Elton Road, Tyndall's Park.

Iguana. A sculpture by Julian Warren, 89 Whiteladies Road, Clifton (Bar Humbug).

Jaguar. The famous ®Jaguar symbol. Hartwell garage, Bath Road, Brislington.

Jellyfish. The Creation plaque by Walter Ritchie, 1986, Bristol Eye Hospital, Lower Maudlin Street.

Jellyfish. On the obelisk 'Unknown Deep' by Philippa Threlfall and Kennedy Collings, 1991, Redcliffe Quay, opposite the Welsh Back end of King Street.

Kangaroo. There is even baby Roo. The Creation plaque by Walter Ritchie, 1986, Bristol Eye Hospital, Lower Maudlin Street.

Kangaroo. Frieze above entrance to Bristol Zoo Gardens, Clifton Down Road, Clifton.

Kiwi. 83 West Town Lane, Brislington.

Lamb. Above a shop on St Mark's Road, Easton.

Leopard. Head of a leopard on a bench end. The leopard's head and front quarters form the arms and legs for Bristol Corporation park benches on the Green at Horfield Road, Kingsdown (these came here from Temple Church Gardens, perhaps they have a better view from here).

Lion and Unicorn. Supporting the Royal Coat of Arms, The RWA, Queen's Road, Clifton. One of the many books in the Bodleian Library in Oxford that are more than 700 years old is the *Ormsby Psalter*. The book has a drawing showing a young maiden trying to protect a unicorn from a hunter.

The enmity that exists between the lion and the unicorn is an allegory for the historic rivalry between Scotland and England. Another early book, the *Faerie Queene* written in 1590 by Edmund Spenser, also tells of this struggle. Before the union of Scotland with England in 1603 the Scottish gold coins had two unicorns as seen on their Royal Coast of Arms, and later the Scottish Unicorn was incorporated into the British Coats of Arms with the lion taking the place of the Welsh Dragon.

Lions. Door knockers on doors of The Exchange, Corn Street.

Lion. Fountain outlet of King George V Memorial Fountain outside Broad Quay House, on the city centre. The lion fountain spout is of aluminium cast, by Bush and Wilton of Bitton.

Lion. On a roof ridge, almshouse, Berkeley Place, Clifton Hill.

Lion. A courageous lion in Victoria Street.

Lion. Head rosettes on cenotaph lamp standards, Colston Avenue.

Lion. Left-hand lion of a pair at the Victoria Rooms, Clifton. Sculptor Henry Poole, 1917.

Lion. Watching the people on the zebra crossing. Right-hand lion of a pair at the Victoria Rooms. Clifton. Sculptor Henry Poole, 1917.

Lion. A very smug-looking lion, I wonder

why? University Road frontage of Browns Restaurant, 38 Queen's Road, Clifton.

Lions. Frontage of the former Drill Hall, Old Market Street.

Lion. Yawning – too much prep?, roof parapet of Clifton College, Guthrie Road, Clifton.

Lizard. Eating grapes, beside the arch in wall nearest the altar of the Elder Lady Chapel, Bristol Cathedral. This very new-looking carving is over 700 years old.

Lynx. Frieze above entrance to Bristol Zoo Gardens, Clifton Down Road, Clifton.

Maybug. By Julian Warren, metal sculptor, above a shop, Princess Victoria Street, Clifton.

Mayfly. The Creation plaque by Walter Ritchie, 1986, Bristol Eye Hospital, Lower Maudlin Street.

Mermaid. The poor mermaid is being attacked by two horrible monsters who are trying to pull off her scales. There are 27 other similar carvings that date to the early 1500s and which are hidden beneath the lift-up seats known as misericords, in the choir stalls of Bristol Cathedral. The Cathedral bookshop has a guide to the carvings and a postcard of some of them.

Mermaids. On a wall of a building in Tailors' Court, off Broad Street.

Mermaid. Merchant Venturers' coat of arms, Merchant Seamen's Almshouses, King Street.

Mice. Pet shop menagerie, 27a East Street, Bedminster.

Millipede. The Creation plaque by Walter Ritchie, 1986, Bristol Eye Hospital, Lower Maudlin Street.

> **Q12** How many legs has the millipede in this plaque got?

Mongoose. The Creation plaque by Walter Ritchie, 1986, Bristol Eye Hospital, Lower Maudlin Street.

Monkey. Holding a cat's paw in the fire, illustrating one of Jean de la Fontaine's fables. Above ground-floor windows, 9–11 Elmdale Road, Tyndall's Park, Clifton.

Monkey. 'Americas' plaque above the west entrance, The Exchange.

Monkey. Judging a wolf and a fox. Above ground-floor windows, 9–11 Elmdale Road, Tyndall's Park.

Monkey. Plaster frieze wall in the stairwell, Royal Fort House, Tyndall Avenue, Clifton.

Monkey. With a sad expression, on a pillar, University Road frontage of Browns Restaurant, 38 Queen's Road, Clifton.

Monkey. Above a shop frontage, Woolcot Road, Redland.

Mosquito. Metal sculpture by Julian Warren, on his railings at 18 Burlington Road, Redland.

Mosquito. The Creation plaque by Walter Ritchie, 1986, Bristol Eye Hospital, Lower Maudlin Street.

Nautilus. Metal sculpture by Julian Warren, on his railings at 18 Burlington Road, Redland.

Octopus. On the obelisk 'Unknown Deep' by Philippa Threlfall and Kennedy Collings, 1991, Redcliffe Quay, opposite the Welsh Back end of King Street.

Octopus. Metal sculpture by Julian Warren, on his railings at 18 Burlington Road, Redland.

Octopus. Watching you from beneath the fountain in the front of the Victoria Rooms, Clifton.

Ostrich. 'Africa' plaque above the south entrance of The Exchange, Corn Street.

Ostrich. Frieze above entrance to Bristol Zoo Gardens, Clifton Down Road, Clifton.

Owl. c.1901, above shops in Woolcot Road, Redland.

Owl. In a frieze, above shops, Cotham Hill.

Owl. c.1901, above shops in Woolcot Road, Redland.

Owl. In a frieze, above shops, Cotham Hill.

Owl. Watching out for pigeons on the parapet of the roof of 130 High Street, Staple Hill (the Portcullis pub).

Owl. On the roof edge of Old Barn, 22 Luccombe Hill, Lower Redland Road, Redland.

Owl. Guiding the Goddess of Wisdom. This classical sculpture in the pediment above the Victoria Rooms, Clifton depicts a flying owl guiding Athena in a chariot driven by Apollo. Also in the same group, 'Night' clasps an owl in her right hand. You will need binoculars to see the detail.

Panther. Frieze above entrance to Bristol Zoo Gardens, Clifton Down Road, Clifton.

Parrot. 'Americas' plaque above the west entrance to The Exchange. This looks like it could be 'Paragon' the mischievous parrot from Rumi's Tales.

Parrots. Pet shop menagerie, 27a East Street, Bedminster.

Pegasus. The winged horse of mythology. Very appropriately this larger-than-life statue can be seen on Filton House (built in 1936), the former headquarters of the Bristol Aeroplane Company at Filton. With mergers and acquisitions over the years, the company went through a number of name changes and subsequently became the British Aerospace Company before the aircraft sector became Airbus UK. When the centre of local operations moved to the airfield, this site became abandoned, awaiting development.

Pelican. On a pillar on the frontage of Browns Restaurant, 38 Queen's Road, Clifton.

Pelican. A symbol of piety feeding young, St Mary Redcliffe Church, North Porch, Redcliffe.

Pelicans. With young, above both sides of door, Crusader House, St Stephen's Street.

Penguin. A strange eighteenth-century interpretation of a penguin eating a fish, on the 'Americas' plaque above the west entrance to The Exchange.

Phoenix. With young. Redcliffe Way near roundabout, opposite North Porch of St Mary Redcliffe Church, Redcliffe.

Pig. High above the memorial fountain, Stoke Road, Durdham Down.

Pig. A Sow, The Creation plaque by Walter Ritchie, 1986, Bristol Eye Hospital, Lower Maudlin Street.

Pigeon. Above a shop front on Woolcot Road, Redland.

Pyramid of animals. Above a pet shop, Pets Plus, 27a East Street, Bedminster.

Quetzal. On gate at 81g Pembroke Road, Clifton. This is the national bird of the Mayans (now Guatemala). It is a rain forest bird, and although you wouldn't realise it from looking at Julian Warren's black metal sculpture on the gate, in real life the bird is very colourful. The male bird's body is an intense emerald and golden green with red belly and white under tail. Its body measures about 38cm but the tail, rich in iridescent blues and greens above and subtle white below, can extend as much as 76cm. This is yet another creature threatened by the destruction of the rain forest habitat.

Rabbits. With babies, upper window panels, 9–11 Elmdale Road, Tyndall's Park.

Ram. On a pillar on the front of Browns Restaurant, 38 Queen's Road, Clifton.

Ram. The head of a ram high above the memorial fountain, Stoke Road, Durdham Down.

Rams. The heads of rams, watching from the roof of the portico of Freemasons Hall, Park Street.

Ram. Playing a medieval instrument that

Raven and Snake. Depiction of one of Aesop's fables, above ground-floor windows, 9–11 Elmdale Road, Tyndall's Park, Clifton.

Rhinoceros. Frieze above entrance to Bristol Zoo Gardens, Clifton Down Road, Clifton.

Scorpion. The Creation plaque by Walter Ritchie, 1986, Bristol Eye Hospital, Lower Maudlin Street.

Scorpion. On the frontage arch of old Pro-Cathedral (now derelict), Park Place, Clifton.

Seagull. Weathervane in gardens opposite Alma Tavern, Alma Vale Road, Clifton.

Sea Horses (or Hippocampi – there are two). Council House, College Green.

Sea Horses. Even though these look like wyverns (two-legged dragons), they are sea horses (see 'Wyvern'). These are above the entrance to QEH gates, Lower Berkeley Road. The pair supporting the school coat of arms show that it was granted by Queen Elizabeth I on March 21 1590.

Sea Horse. Hiding and peering at you from under the fountain at the Victoria Rooms, Clifton. Sculptor Henry Poole, 1917.

Seal. Catching lunch at the fountain outside the Victoria Rooms, Clifton. Sculptor Henry Poole, 1917.

Serpent of the Sea. On the obelisk 'Unknown Deep', by Philippa Threlfall and Kennedy Collings, 1991, Redcliffe Quay, opposite the Welsh Back end of King Street.

Sheep. The head of a sheep high above the memorial fountain, Stoke Road, Durdham Down.

Sheep. Newly-covered in gold leaf above Sheepdrove Organic Butchers, 3 Lower Redland Road, Redland.

Sheep. Dozing above fire mantle, Royal Fort House, Tyndall Avenue.

Sheep. A plaque by Philippa Threlfall and Kennedy Collings, representing the wool trade, Colston Street.

Sheep. Plaster frieze, stairwell, Royal Fort House, Tyndall Avenue, Clifton.

Sheep. On the Fleece pub sign, Wool Hall, St Thomas Street.

Slug. The slug is on a leash, with a pack on its back, and is being led by a man. It is followed by another man with a whip. In olden times when goods were moved by mules that walked so slowly, they were sometimes known as 'Slugs'. This carving, a medieval cartoon in wood, is one of 28 similar carvings that date to the early 1500s and which are hidden beneath the lift-up seats known as misericords, in the choir stalls of Bristol Cathedral. A four-page guide to the carvings is available in the Cathedral bookshop.

Snail. The Creation plaque by Walter Ritchie, 1986, Bristol Eye Hospital, Lower Maudlin Street.

Snake. One of six snakes on balcony brackets at Cotham Road, opposite Highbury Chapel.

Snakes. Balcony brackets, rear of Anglesea Place, Clifton.

Snake. On a seat at Bristol Grammar School, Woodland Road.

Sphinx. Right-hand one of pair, above a door of St Vincent's Priory, Sion Hill, Clifton. The sphinx shown here is likely to be the Greek sphinx, part woman, part lion, and with wings of an eagle.

Spider. In a web. The Creation plaque by Walter Ritchie, 1986, Bristol Eye Hospital, Lower Maudlin Street.

Spiny shell. Home to a hermit crab, the fountain at the Victoria Rooms, Clifton.

Squirrel. Upper-window panels, 9–11 Elmdale Road, Tyndall's Park.

Squirrel. Plaster ceiling, Royal Fort House, Tyndall Avenue.

Reindeer. A stag, frieze above entrance to Bristol Zoo Gardens, Clifton Down Road, Clifton.

Starfish. On the obelisk 'Unknown Deep', by Philippa Threlfall and Kennedy Collings, 1991, Redcliffe Quay, opposite the Welsh Back end of King Street.

Stork. Stone frieze above shops in Cotham Hill, Cotham.

Stork. Being tricked by fox, from a fable by Jean de la Fontaine. Above ground-floor windows, second side panel, 11 Elmdale Road, Tyndall's Park.

Swans. Plaster ceiling, Royal Fort House, Tyndall Avenue.

Stork. Entertaining fox to dinner, and getting her revenge, from a fable by Jean de la Fontaine. Above ground-floor windows, first side panel, 11 Elmdale Road, Tyndall's Park.

Terrible creatures with no name (the worst sort). Looking down on you from the roof of Clifton College, Guthrie Road, Clifton.

Tiger. Frieze above entrance to Bristol Zoo Gardens, Clifton Down Road, Clifton.

Tortoise. The Creation plaque by Walter Ritchie, 1986, Bristol Eye Hospital, Lower Maudlin Street.

Tortoise and Hare. One of Aesop's fables, above ground-floor windows, 9–11 Elmdale Road, Tyndall's Park.

Turtle. Victoria Rooms fountain, Clifton. Sculptor Henry Poole, 1917.

Unicorn. King Edward VII Statue, Victoria Rooms, Queen's Road, Clifton.

Unicorn. Bristol's pair of life-size gilded unicorns are on the two end-towers of the Council House, College Green. Each unicorn is 3.6 metres high. They were put there on October 25, 1950, and initially caused outrage because of the cost to the ratepayers of £2,400. Sculpted by David McFall, RA, they represent the supporters on Bristol's common seal, dated 1569, which is still used on very important letters and official documents.

Unicorn. With a broken tail, above the entrance to the old stock exchange, St Nicholas Street.

Unicorn. As a supporter to the royal coat of arms on the Royal West of England Academy, Queen's Road. The poor thing has lost its horn! The unicorn was replaced by the Welsh dragon on the Royal coat of Arms, on instructions from the Scottish King James I (of England) when he forced the Union of Scotland and England in 1607. The doggerel schoolyard rhyme was probably written by William King, author of *Useful Transactions in Philosophy*, which dates to around 1708, and reflected the historic rivalry between Scotland and England.

Unicorns. On the city coat of arms on Victorian lamp posts in Clyde Road, Redland.

Unicorns. On the city coat of arms on Victorian lamp posts in Guthrie Road, Clifton.

Unicorns. On the coat of arms on the railings of Bath Road bridge.

Unicorns. On the coat of arms on a

Victorian lamp post in the Mall, Clifton.

Unicorns. Massive coat of arms above the entrance to the former Drill Hall (converted to housing in 2005), Old Market Street.

Viper fish. With a very bad attitude! Metal sculpture by Julian Warren, on his railings at 18 Burlington Road, Redland.

Very Beastly beasts. Medieval grotesques in the style of the medieval artist Hieronymous Bosch decorating the pillars outside the North Porch of St Mary Redcliffe Church.

Wolf. Eating a sheep, while the shepherd sleeps. Arch in wall of Elder Lady Chapel, Bristol Cathedral.

Wolf. With a fox, both are being judged by a monkey (fox on the left, wolf on the right), above ground-floor windows, 9–11 Elmdale Road, Tyndall's Park.

Woodpecker. Knocking to get in? 59 Apsley Road, Clifton (Rucola Restaurant) by sculptor Julian Warren.

Whale. Killer whale, Bristol Scuba Centre, 267 West Street, Bedminster.

Whale. This is the only work that we broke the rules for because, although it's not a 3D representation, we thought it was worth telling you about. The mural, by Masters and Milne, is opposite the Nova Scotia pub, Nova Scotia Place.

Wyvern. A two-legged dragon. Look out for this fabulous beast, a winged dragon with the feet and claws of an eagle, and a serpent-like barbed tail. It was originally the badge of the ancient Kingdom of Mercia (Bristol was a border town between Mercia and Wessex). The wyvern was also adopted for the badge of the 2nd Earl Thomas Lancaster of Leicester, and much later in the nineteenth century it was also used by the Midland railway companies.

We hope that you have enjoyed this adventure and have seen lots of exciting creatures around our city that you didn't know about.

There are still lots and lots of creatures that are not in this book – have fun discovering them for yourselves! Don't forget to visit the Beastly Bristol website for loads of pictures of the Bristol menagerie.

http://spaces.msn.com/beastlybristol

Quiz answers

1. Bedminster Pet Shop. There are five different sorts of pets.

2. Bedminster Pet Shop. The pyramid is made up of 20 creatures balancing on each other, 19 of which appear in the picture.

3. Tailors' Court, above the doorway. The ten items are: two camels, a lion, a lamb (Agnus Dei – the Lamb of God), a knight's armour, a cherub and the head of St John the Baptist, a tent and two finely made ermine trimmed (white fur with dark spots) cloaks.

4. King's Arcade, Boyce's Avenue. There are 48 dragons on balcony brackets.

5. Victoria Rooms, Clifton. The lion on the left-hand side is snarling, but the other lion has its mouth shut.

6. 14 lions, all along the front of the former Drill Hall (converted to housing in 2005), Old Market Street.

7. The unicorn on the Royal West of England Academy, Queen's Road. The poor thing has lost its horn, so is it now just a horse?

8. Sphinx above the door of the house named St Vincent's Priory, Sion Hill. The answer to the riddle 'What is the animal that has four feet in the morning, two at mid-day and three in the evening?' correctly answered by Oedipus is 'Man. Because in infancy he crawls on all fours, at maturity walks on two legs and in old age two legs but with the aid of a stick'.

9. The Creation plaque by Walter Ritchie, 1986, Bristol Eye Hospital, Lower Maudlin Street. We counted 23 different sorts of creatures in the last plaque.

10. Baldwin Street. Above the entrance to number 18a there are four bees and their beehive.

11. The statue used to have railings around it. It has also been turned around to face the other way. When the square was turned back into a park in 2004, they turned him to face the city centre, as he was originally.

12. The millipede in The Creation plaque by Walter Ritchie, 1986, Bristol Eye Hospital, Lower Maudlin Street. How close did you get to 79 legs? And don't forget to double this to give the total of 158.

Some animal addresses – a challenge!

You are invited to find even more creatures. Here is a list of streets and districts in Bristol that are named after creatures. Often the street names tell us about long-lost field names and give us clues to what the countryside was like before the city that we live in was built. See if you can identify the reason for their names. The answers are not in this book, but to start you off I have provided a clue to at least one place with an interesting beastly story, Dragonswell Road, in Henbury and the pond that never froze. (The answer is in the Dragon section of the index.) I will leave you to discover the reasons for these others. Be careful though, not all are as obvious as they seem.

Bull Lane, BS2.
Centaurus Road, BS12.
Cock Road, BS15.
Crane Close, BS15.
Curlew Close, BS16.
Deerhurst, BS15.
Deerswood, BS15.
Dolphin Street, BS1.
Dove Lane, BS5.
Dove Street, BS1.
Dragon Walk, BS5.
Dragonswell Road, BS10.
Drake Road, BS3.
Duckmoor Road, BS3.
Eagle Road, BS4.
Emmett Wood, BS14.
Ermine Way, BS9.
Falcon Close, BS9.
Falcon Close, BS12.
Falcondale Road, BS9.
Fishponds, BS16.
Fox Close, BS4.
Fox Court, BS15.
Fox House, BS4.
Fox Road, BS5.
Foxcombe Road, BS14.
Foxcote, BS15.
Foxcroft Road, BS5.
Frog Lane, BS1.
Frogmore Street, BS1.
Gooseland Close, BS14.
Grayling House, BS9.
Hawkfield Close, BS13.
Hawksbury Road, BS16.
Hawksmoor Close, BS14.
Heron Road, BS5.
Kestrel Close, BS9.
Kite Hay Close BS16.
Lamb Street, BS2.
Lapwing Gardens, BS16.
Lark's Field, BS16.
Larkleaze Road, BS15.
Linnet BS12.
Magpie Bottom Lane, BS15.
Magpie Bottom Lane, BS5.
Merlin Close, BS9.
Merlin Road, BS12.
Nags Head, BS5.
Nuthatch Drive, BS16.
Osprey Court, BS5.
Osprey Road, BS5.
Otterford Close, BS14.
Owls Head Road, BS15.
Oxleaze Lane, BS13.
Pegasus Road, BS12.
Phoenix Grove, BS6.
Ravenhead Drive, BS14.
Ravens Court, BS12.
Ravens Wood, BS15.
Ravenswood Road, BS6.
Sheeps Croft, BS13.
Sheepwood Close, BS10.
St. Stephen's Street, BS1 (this is difficult one – but it really does have a creature connection – honest!)
Swallow Drive, BS12.
Swanmoor Crescent, BS10.
Whinchat Gardens, BS16.
Wolfridge Gardens, BS10.

Further Reading

Many of the creatures you will find on our Beastly trail around Bristol have inspired poets and writers for hundreds of years. You might already know a lot of the characters, such as Kaa the Rock Python from Rudyard Kipling's *The Jungle Book*, A.A. Milne's Winnie the Pooh, Kanga and Roo, and all the strange creatures that Alice met on her *Adventures in Wonderland*, but there are even more to read about.

We have included this small selection of the many books and poems that include animals so that you too can find out more about the antics and adventures of the creatures in this book.

Animals

Armadillo: The Beginning of the Armadillos, in *Just So Stories*, by Rudyard Kipling.

Bear: The story of Baloo, in *The Jungle Book*, by Rudyard Kipling.

Bee: 'Julius Caesar and the Honey-bee', a poem by Charles Tennyson Turner.

Camel: 'The Camel' a poem by Carmen de Gasztold (translated from the French by Rumer Godden).

Centaur: Firenze, Bane, Magorian from the Harry Potter stories by J.K. Rowling.

Dragon: 'Glaurung – the father of the dragons. The Urboki created by Morgoth in Angband, The bane of men & dwarves', in *Lord of the Rings* and *Silmarillion*, by J. R. R. Tolkien.

Dragonfly: 'Today I saw the dragonfly', a poem by Alfred, Lord Tennyson.

Elephant: 'The fable of the Elephant & the seven blind men of Hindustan', Indian fables of Pilpay. Pilpay was an ancient Indian Bramin philosopher who, like the Greek Aesop, also wrote fables. 62 of his fables were translated into English and published in London in 1775.

Fish: 'To a Fish', a poem by James Henry Leigh Hunt – 'You strange, astonished-looking, angle-faced ...'. Also, his 'A Fish answers'.

Hedgehog: 'February', a poem from *The Shepherds Calendar*, by John Clare – 'The hedgehog in his hollow root, sees the woodmoss clear of straw & hunts the hedge for fuller fruit...'

Horses: *Black Beauty* by Anna Sewell.

Kangaroo (and baby): Kanga and Roo, from the stories of Winnie the Pooh, by A. A. Milne. There is also the poem 'Kangaroo', by D.H. Lawrence – 'In the northern hemisphere, life seems to leap at the air...'

Lions: There are lots of stories and poems about lions; Simba, The Lion King; Aslan, in *The Lion, The Witch and the Wardrobe* by C.S. Lewis; the cowardly lion in *The Wizard of Oz*; or even Alex, the lion king of Central Park Zoo, New York, from the film *Madagascar*.

Monkey: Abu in the story of *Aladdin*.

Mouse: 'To a mouse on turning her up in her nest with the plough', a poem by Robert Burns – '...Wee, sleekit, cowr'n, timorous, beastie'.

Owl: From the stories of Winnie the Pooh, by A. A. Milne, and of course Harry Potter's personal mail owl, Hedwig, from the Harry Potter stories by J. K. Rowling.

Parrots: Iago in the story of *Aladdin*. Also the story of the very cheeky 'Paragon the Parrot', one of Rumi's tales. Rumi was a poet and mystic from Afghanistan who went to live in Turkey in the 1400s. An English translation of his tales is available.

Penguins: Skipper, Kowalski and Rio, the fugitives from Central Park Zoo, New York, in the film *Madagascar*.

Phoenix: *Harry Potter and the Order of the Phoenix* by J. K. Rowling.

Books

a Bristol Eye: The city seen from new perspectives, Stephen Morris and Tim Mowl, Redcliffe Press, Bristol, 2001.

Æsop: The Complete Fables, Penguin Classics, 1998.

The Castle of Dragalno, Book 1 of the Dragon Trilogy, by Owen Elloway Smith. Publisher: P Elloway Smith, 10 Falloden Road, Bristol BS9 4HR. Published in support of the Hands Around The World, Orphanage Project.

'The Fables of La Fontaine' in *Masterpieces of Foreign Literature* translated from the French, by E. Wright, Jnr., 1866.

The Instructive and Entertaining Fables of Pilpay, an Ancient Indian Philosopher, printed for J & F Rivington (and several others), London MDCCLXXV, (1775).

New Larousse Encyclopedia of Mythology, introduction by Robert Graves, Hamlyn, 1959

Out of the Ark: An Anthology of Animal Verse, compiled by Gwendolyn Reed, Longman Young Books, 1968.

The Paragon Parrot and other inspirational tales of Wisdom, tales from Rumi, retold by Arthur Scholey, Watkins Publishing, London, 2002.

Sculpture in Bristol, Douglas Merritt, Redcliffe Press, Bristol, 2002.

The Street Names of Bristol: Their origins and meanings, Veronica Smith, Broadcast Books, Bristol, 2001.

Websites

There is an exciting website **www.poetryarchive.co.uk** – set up by the Poet Laureate Andrew Motion – that brings some of the poems into your own home or school. If you have a look at the Children's Archive page, you will see that poems have been sorted into different themes, including animals. You can download poems about some of the animals we have seen and some poems are even recorded by the poets, so that you can listen to them as well.

Don't forget that we will also be adding to our picture gallery of creatures on **http://spaces.msn.com/beastlybristol** as we discover them and you can also email us your own discoveries to **info@childrensbristol.co.uk** or via our website **www.childrensbristol.co.uk**

Other useful sites:

www.wwf.org.uk

www.iucn.org

www.extinct.petermaas.nl

www.travellog.com/guatemala/quetzal.html

www.bristolzoo.org.uk

Acknowledgements

Douglas Merritt, for sharing with us his knowledge of all things statuesque in Bristol.
Kevin Powell, who produced the splendid caricatures of the zanier beasts. Meera Joshi, for the rhymes that bought our alphabet to life. Astrid and Charles Pestel, for arranging for the reinstatement of Michael Q Smith's canary. Julian P Warren, the sculptor for his continuing production of an amazing metal menagerie (it seemed at times faster than we could record them). John Wyatt, for his carving of Gromit (we hope he doesn't have too long a wait for Wallace). Stephen Crabbe, for introducing me to the overlooked medieval animal delights within Bristol Cathedral and the parish church of St Mary Redcliffe ('The fairest, goodliest and most famous parish church in England'). Oliver Ledbury, for finding and photographing what must be the largest and most colourful caterpillar in the land, and to the children of Victoria Park Infants School who take care of it. Derek and Janet Fisher of *Bygone Bristol* for finding the old picture of the king on his horse. Veronica Smith, whose research helped to identify Bristol's zoomorphic place names, Barbara Drummond for providing information on the religious significance of some of the carved creatures. Audrey Fussell, Gillian Baxter, Joan Soloman, Jacqueline Pearce, Graham Morris, Phil and Sarah Gregory, Jenny Holt, and many others who have encouraged and supported this project. Lastly, but by no means least Diane my wife, who as well as helping to research the historic backgrounds, also waited patiently on our walks around Bristol while I often stopped to photograph yet another discovery.

We should remember to thank all the clever and gifted artists and sculptors who made all the wonderful animals, and not to forget the people who had them installed around Bristol for our enjoyment. Maybe having seen all these, one day you yourself will make a creature to add to our city's wondrous collection of creatures.

The Children's Bristol Series
www.childrensbristol.co.uk

Children's Bristol

Edited by John Sansom

This new, expanded edition of Bristol's best loved family guide is essential reading for anyone with children to bring up or entertain. Its opening chapters outline Bristol's fascinating history and its great maritime heritage. There are chapters on things to do, bright ideas for children's parties, family outings, places to visit in and around the city, to a radius of about 40 miles.

There are special chapters on animals and birds, historic places, museums, Roman remains, caves and even where to look for ghosts.

288 pages and fantastic value at £8.50.

24 Family Walks in and around Bristol

Lesley Turney

The walks in this latest Children's Bristol Guide have been devised especially for families of all ages. All are located within easy distance of Bristol and vary in length and difficulty, from the toddler- and buggy-friendly stretches of the Bristol-Bath Cycle and Walkway to the stiffish ascent of Cadbury Camp. Easy directions, an interesting and sometimes educational commentary, photographs and maps – all add up to the best family walking book in Bristol.

112 pages and great value at only £6.95.

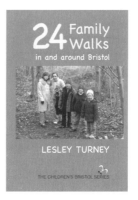

Children's Hospice South West

All our guides support this great charity. For every copy of *Children's Bristol* sold, we are donating 75p to the hospice; and 25p for every copy sold of *Beastly Bristol* and *24 Family Walks in and around Bristol*.